Andrew Jackson &
Sam Patch Jackson

Zachary Taylor & horse

Teddy Roosevelt Jr. &
Eli Yale Roosevelt

Calvin & Grace Coolidge with dog

Benjamin Harrison's grandchildren
with Old Whiskers

To Mr. Donovan, and in memory of Dusty, my best dog friend.

Thank you to Andrew Hagar and Tricia Rogalski at the
Presidential Pet Museum for their assistance.

Front endpaper photo credits, Row 1 (L to R): *Theodore Roosevelt's pet one-legged rooster,* Library of Congress, LC-DIG-ppmsca-36498 [P&P]; *Blackie & Tiger, 10/20/23,*
Library of Congress, LC-DIG-npcc-09707 [P&P]; *Major General Andrew Jackson, President of the United States, painted by Thomas Sully, engraved by James B. Longacre,* Library of Congress,
LC-DIG-pga-07371 [P&P]; *Major-General Zachary Taylor—President of the United States, from an original daguerreotype engraved by John Sartain,* Library of Congress, LC-DIG-pga-02632 [P&P];
Teddy, Jr. & "Eli Yale," photographer Frances Benjamin Johnston, Library of Congress, LC-USZ62-17184 [P&P]; **Front, Row 2 (L to R):** *White House Sheep on Lawn,* photographer Harris &
Ewing, Library of Congress, LC-DIG-hec-10789 [P&P]; *Kermit Roosevelt and his dog Jack,* photographer Frances Benjamin Johnston, Library of Congress, LC-DIG-ds-09843 [P&P]; *President
Coolidge and Mrs. Coolidge with dog outside White House, Washington, D.C.,* photographer Harris & Ewing, Library of Congress, LC-DIG-hec-34577 [P&P]; *White House—Major Russell Harrison and
Harrison children—Baby McKee and sister on goat cart,* photographer Frances Benjamin Johnston, Library of Congress, LC-USZ62-118058 [P&P]; **Back endpaper photo credits, Row 1
(L to R):** *General Grant's horse "Cincinnati,"* Library of Congress, LC-DIG-stereo-1s02751 [P&P]; *Mrs. Coolidge at garden party, 6/3/26,* Library of Congress, LC-DIG-npcc-15926 [P&P]; *Mr. and Mrs.
Theodore Roosevelt with children and dog, some seated, others standing, outdoors,* photographer Pach Brothers, N.Y., Library of Congress, LC-DIG-ppmsca-35755 [P&P]; *White House possum, 5/25/29,*
Library of Congress, LC-DIG-npcc-17484 [P&P]; **Back, Row 2 (L to R):** *Mrs. Coolidge exhibits her pet raccoon Rebecca to crowds of children gathered for Easter egg rolling,* Library of Congress,
LC-USZ62-131302 [P&P]; *Gen. Grant's horse,* published by Bain News Service, Library of Congress, LC DIG ggbain 10392 [P&P]; *President Roosevelt's dogs (no. 2),* Library of Congress,
LC-DIG-ppmsca-36493 [P&P]; *Pauline, pet cow of President Taft on lawn, in front of the State, War and Navy Building, Washington, D.C.,* Library of Congress, LC-USZ62-94731 [P&P].

The text of this book is set in 15-point Celestia Antique.
The illustrations were rendered in cut paper, ink, gouache, marker, and colored pencil.

MANUFACTURED IN CHINA

1 3 5 7 9 10 8 6 4 2

First Edition

If you want a friend in Washington

Erin McGill

schwartz & wade books · new york

As the president, you are in charge of the WHOLE of the United States of America. That is a lot of responsibility.

Citizens might not agree with your opinions, ideas, or political party. Whether Whig, Federalist, Republican, Democrat, or Independent, many presidents hoped for a reliable and steadfast friend.

President Harry S. Truman
once famously said,

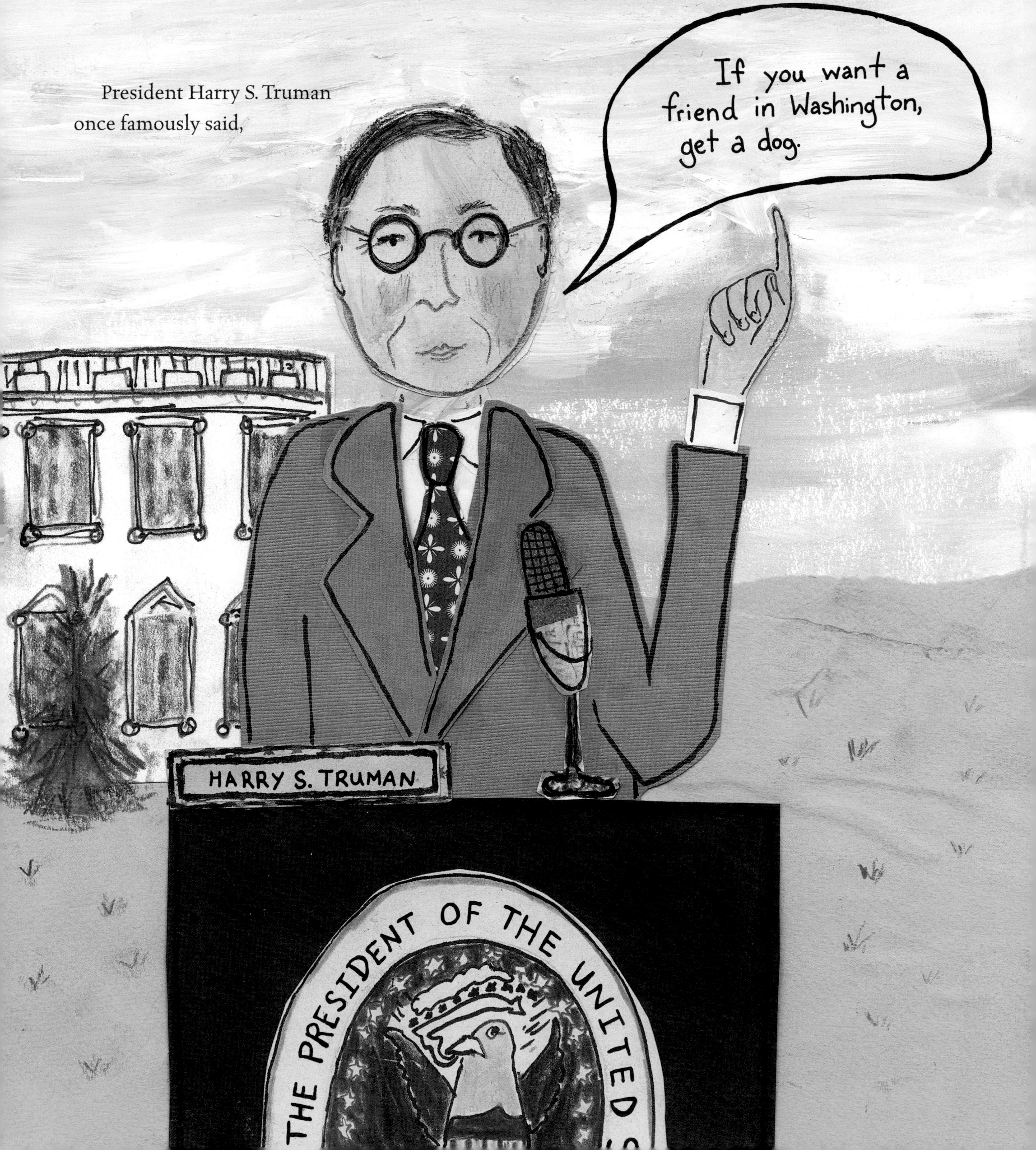

And a dog is what many presidents got.

Lady, Forester, Drunkard, Mopsey, Cloe, Captain, Taster, Rover, Tipler, Vulcan, Sweet Lips, Tipsy & Searcher Washington

Juno & Satan Adams (J.Q.)

Monroe's dog

Le Beau Tyler

Punch Buchanan

King Cole Coolidge

Tyler's wolfhounds

Lara Buchanan

Bruce Wilson

Pierce's pups

Otis Hayes

Tiny Tim Coolidge

Hector Cleveland

Blaze Roosevelt (F.D.)

Peter Pan Coolidge

Jip Lincoln

Rosie Grant

Juno & Shep Hayes

Veto Garfield

Big Ben Hoover

Blackjack Roosevelt (T.)

Pat Hoover

Dot Hayes

Fido Lincoln

Grim Hayes

Faithful Grant

Skip Roosevelt (T.)

Tiny Roosevelt (F.D.)

Meggie Roosevelt (F.D.)

President Roosevelt (F.D.)

Cleveland's dogs

Caruso Taft

Duke & Hector Hayes

Feller & Mike Truman

Winks Roosevelt (F.D.)

Jet Hayes

Fala Roosevelt (F.D.)

Rollo Roosevelt (T.)

Manchu Roosevelt (T.)

Cleveland's other dogs

Major Roosevelt (F.D.)

Dash Harrison (B.)

Sailor Boy Roosevelt (T.)

Pete Roosevelt (T.)

Davie Wilson

Old Boy Harding

Laddie Boy Harding

Liberty & Misty Ford

Lucky Ford

Palo Alto Coolidge

Calamity Jane Coolidge

Boston Beans Coolidge

Blackberry Coolidge

Prudence Prim & Rob Roy Coolidge

Bessie Coolidge

Ruby Rouch Coolidge

Paul Pry Coolidge

Patrick Hoover

Sonny Hoover

Weejie Hoover

King Tut Hoover

Glen Hoover

Eaglehurst Gillette Hoover

Yukon Hoover

Rex & Peggy Reagan

Taca Reagan

Fuzzy & Victory Reagan

Clipper Kennedy

Lucky Reagan

Lewis Brown Carter

Grits Carter

Heidi Eisenhower

Charlie Kennedy

Wolf Kennedy

Gaullie Kennedy

Shannon Kennedy

Barney Bush (G.W.)

Yuki & Blanco Johnson (L.B.)

Miss Beazley Bush (G.W.)

King Timahoe, Pasha & Vicky Nixon

Buddy Clinton

Him, Her, Edgar & Freckles Johnson (L.B.)

Pushinka, Butterfly, White Tips, Blackie & Streaker Kennedy

Millie & Ranger Bush (G.H.W.)

Spot Bush (G.W.)

Bo & Sonny Obama

Plenty of presidents found a friend in Fido. Abraham Lincoln's dog was actually named Fido, which is Latin for "trust in" or "confidence in." But Lincoln thought life in Washington might be too stressful for Fido, so when he was elected, he found Fido a new home with a close friend.

Fala, Franklin D. Roosevelt's dog, held the esteemed title of honorary private in the U.S. Army.

George H. W. Bush's dog, Millie, wrote a book for the First Lady, Barbara. After Millie passed away, the Bushes showed their gratitude by dedicating a dog park to her in Hou..., Texas, affectionately naming it the Millie Bush Bark Park.

Millie's Book for Barbara

Barack Obama's dog, Bo, did not write a book for his owner. But there were plush toys created of him. Everyone could snuggle with Bo.

President Truman didn't follow his own advice. When a supporter from Missouri sent him a cocker spaniel named Feller, he quickly gave him away. Maybe a dog was not the kind of friend he had in mind.

If you want a friend in Washington, maybe you should get a cat.

And a cat is what many presidents got.

Van Buren's tiger cubs

Miss Pussy Hayes

Tabby & Dixie Lincoln

Piccolomini Hayes

1st Siamese cat in America

Siam Hayes

The Adventures of Mark Twain

Valeriano Weyler & Enrique DeLome McKinley

Tom Quartz Roosevelt (T.)

Slippers Roosevelt (T.)

Puffins & Mittens Wilson

Shan Ford

Blacky Coolidge

Tiger Coolidge

Socks Clinton

Misty Malarky Ying Yang Carter

India Bush (G.W.)

Tom Kitten Kennedy

The first cats to take residency in the White House belonged to President Lincoln. He loved to rescue strays. Legend has it he liked talking to them.

Dixie is smarter than my whole cabinet, and furthermore, she does not talk back.

There were many Siamese cats in the White House. The first to arrive, Siam, was a gift from an American diplomat in Bangkok, Thailand, to President Rutherford B. Hayes.

To: Mr. President
Regards: The American Consul

HANDLE WITH CARE

President Bill Clinton's cat, Socks, enjoyed perching on his owner's shoulders. Socks also did important therapy work, visiting students and senior citizens.

You might think that when you are president, you can keep whatever kind of cats you want. Nope! The Sultan of Oman sent President Martin Van Buren two tiger cubs.

Just as Van Buren was preparing for the tigers' arrival, Congress stepped in.

The tigers were confiscated and sent to a zoo.

If you want a friend in Washington, maybe you should get a more practical pet, like a horse.

And a horse is what many presidents got.

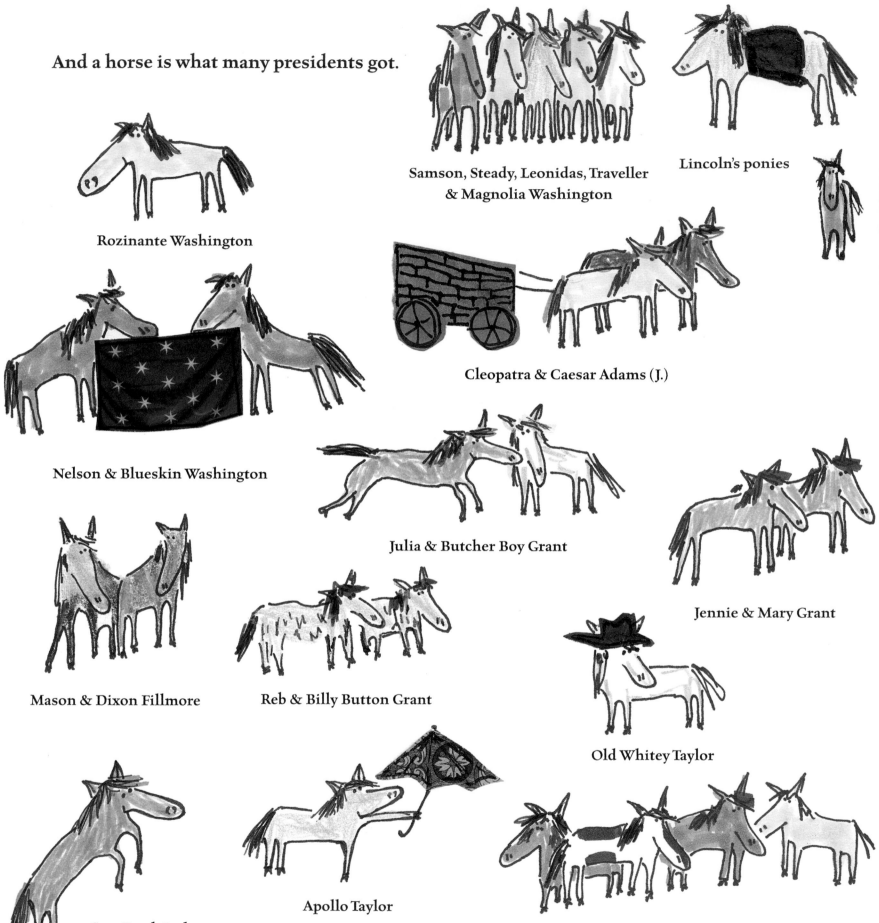

Rozinante Washington

Samson, Steady, Leonidas, Traveller
& Magnolia Washington

Lincoln's ponies

Nelson & Blueskin Washington

Cleopatra & Caesar Adams (J.)

Julia & Butcher Boy Grant

Jennie & Mary Grant

Mason & Dixon Fillmore

Reb & Billy Button Grant

Old Whitey Taylor

Sam Patch Jackson

Apollo Taylor

Emily, Lady Nashville, Bolivia & Thruxton Jackson

Egypt & St. Louis Grant

Cincinnati & Jeff Davis Grant

Hayes's horses

Kit Garfield

Arthur's horses

Cleveland's ponies

Algonquin Roosevelt (T.)

**Bleistein, Renown, Rosewell, Rusty, Jocko Root,
Grey Dawn, Wyoming & Yagenka Roosevelt (T.)**

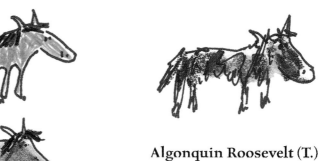

Tex & Leprechaun Kennedy

Judge & General Roosevelt (T.)

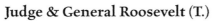

Macaroni Kennedy

The General Tyler

Sardar & Rufus Kennedy

George Washington, our nation's first president, had very bad teeth. He went through many sets of dentures. Washington did not want his horses to suffer the same misfortune. As a result, he had a fastidious tooth-brushing regimen for all of his horses.

Before cars, horses were not just loyal companions, but also modes of transportation. John Adams, the second president and the first to live in the White House, had extravagant taste and built twelve stalls for his horses and their fancy carriages. When Adams did not win reelection, he left his horses and carriages to the incoming president, Thomas Jefferson. Jefferson did not agree with Adams's politics— or with his taste.

First Lady Jackie Kennedy's horse, Sardar, along with pony friends Tex and Macaroni, found themselves in the middle of a scandal when protestors revolted against their wardrobe—or lack thereof. No saddles and shoes? They were completely nude!

Decency today means morality tomorrow!

A NUDE HORSE IS A RUDE HORSE

(The horses, of course, did not care whether they were clothed or not.)

If you want a friend in Washington, maybe you should choose a pet that doesn't require clothing, like a farm animal.

And a farm animal is what many presidents got.

Sukey Harrison (W.H.)

Hayes's goat

Hayes's cows

Old Ike Wilson & Wilson's sheep

Harrison's billy goat (W.H.)

Grant's gamecocks

Nanny & Nanko Lincoln

Pauline Wayne Taft

Mooly Wooly Taft

Old Whiskers Harrison (B.)

Roosevelt's rooster (T.)

McKinley's roosters

Bush's cow (G.W.)

Maude Roosevelt &
Roosevelt's hen (T.)

Cleveland's gamecocks

Jefferson's Sheep

Ebenezer Coolidge

President Woodrow Wilson put his pets to work to help the country during World War I. His flock of sheep nibbled at the White House grounds, keeping the lawns tidy so gardeners could join the war effort.

Selling the sheep's fleece was very lucrative. Some of it was auctioned off to help the Red Cross; some was used to make yarn to create products such as socks for soldiers.

President William Howard Taft enjoyed fresh milk. A senator from Wisconsin thought of the perfect gift for him—a cow. Her name was Pauline Wayne, but fans called her Miss Wayne.

The bovine became very well known and even toured the country. One of her stops was at the International Dairymen's Expo in Milwaukee.

People were so eager to try Miss Wayne's milk that, once, when an agriculturalist spotted her grazing on the White House lawn, he decided to hop the fence and sneak a taste.

If you want a friend in Washington, maybe you should get a bigger animal—one you can't sneak up on.

And a bigger animal is what many presidents got.

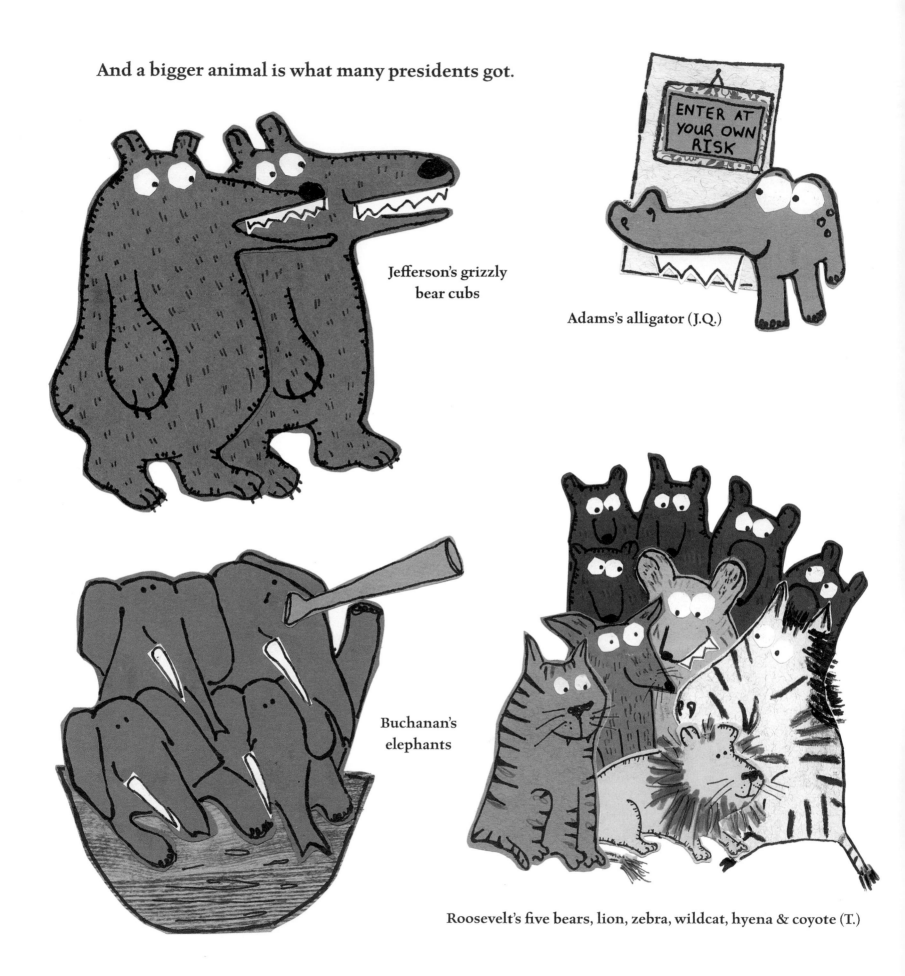

ENTER AT YOUR OWN RISK

Jefferson's grizzly bear cubs

Adams's alligator (J.Q.)

Buchanan's elephants

Roosevelt's five bears, lion, zebra, wildcat, hyena & coyote (T.)

Tax Reduction and
Budget Bureau Coolidge

Coolidge's wallaby

Smoky Coolidge

Billy Coolidge

Coolidge's black bear

Hoover's
alligators

What do you give a president who has everything? An alligator! Legend has it that's what Revolutionary War hero the Marquis de Lafayette thought President John Quincy Adams might like. It is said that Adams kept the alligator in the bathroom and would show it off to his guests.

President Calvin Coolidge was given a pygmy hippo by businessman Harvey Samuel Firestone. Billy, as the hippo was named, was immediately donated to the National Zoo. He became a star exhibit at the 1939 World's Fair, and his descendants can be found today in zoos across America.

The prize for biggest pet goes to a herd of elephants, a gift from the king of Siam to President James Buchanan. The only problem: the elephants never arrived.

When Abraham Lincoln, the next president, got word that the pachyderm parcel was en route, he politely declined the shipment and sent them back.

If you want a friend in Washington, maybe you should get a smaller pet, like a bird.

And a bird is what many presidents got.

Polly Washington

Dick Jefferson

Madison's parrot

Grant's parrot

blah blah blah

Johnny Ty Tyler

Hayes's canaries & mockingbird

Poll Jackson

Pierce's birds

Cleveland's canaries & mockingbirds

Buchanan's bald eagles

Washington Post McKinley

Loretta Roosevelt (T.)

Eli Yale
Roosevelt (T.)

Roosevelt's barn owl (T.)

Wilson's songbirds

Coolidge's
mockingbird

Snowflake Coolidge

Jack Lincoln

Bob & Petey Harding

Old Bill Coolidge

Nip & Tuck Coolidge

Gabby
Eisenhower

Johnson's lovebirds (L.B.)

Enoch Coolidge

Bluebell &
Maybelle Kennedy

Robin Kennedy

Mockingbirds were among the most popular fowl to grace the White House. President Thomas Jefferson had a few of these beautiful birds, but his favorite was called Dick. Dick had free range of the president's office, and Jefferson enjoyed harmonizing with his bird on the violin.

President Abraham Lincoln signed an official proclamation to set aside the last Thursday in November as a "Day of Thanksgiving and Praise."

In honor of the new holiday, someone sent Lincoln a turkey. Lincoln's son, Tad, took a liking to it. He named the bird Jack and taught it to follow him around.

One day, Tad and Jack interrupted a meeting to beg his father to save his new friend from becoming holiday dinner. Jack was the first turkey to be pardoned, beginning a Thanksgiving tradition that continues today.

President Andrew Jackson owned an African grey parrot named Poll that had a filthy mouth. The president and Poll went everywhere together.

Unfortunately, Poll outlived Jackson and attended his owner's funeral—and he had a few things to say!

If you want a friend in Washington, maybe you should get a quieter, smaller critter.

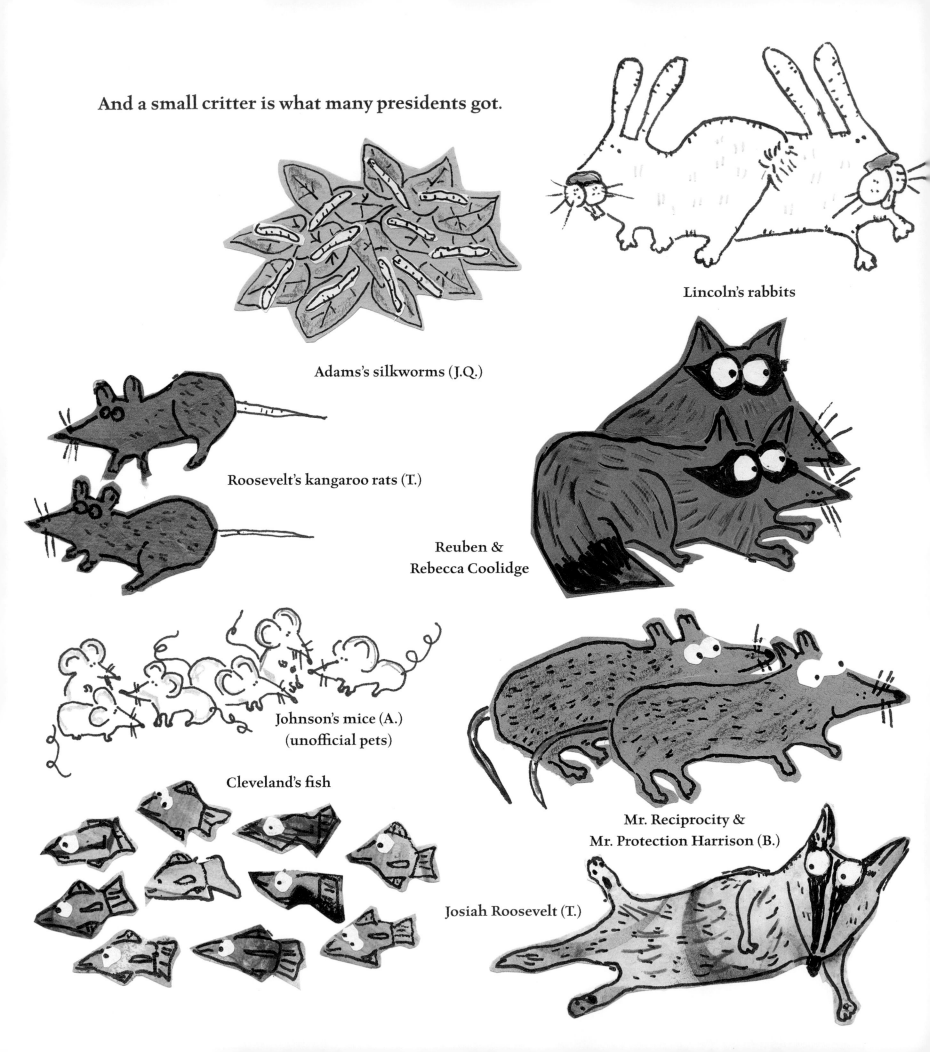

And a small critter is what many presidents got.

Lincoln's rabbits

Adams's silkworms (J.Q.)

Roosevelt's kangaroo rats (T.)

Reuben &
Rebecca Coolidge

Johnson's mice (A.)
(unofficial pets)

Cleveland's fish

Mr. Reciprocity &
Mr. Protection Harrison (B.)

Josiah Roosevelt (T.)

Emily Spinach Roosevelt (T.)

Other Roosevelt snakes (T.)

Peter Roosevelt (T.)

Johnson's hamsters (L.B.)

Roosevelt's flying squirrels (T.)

Pete Harding

Bill Roosevelt (T.)

Admiral Dewey, Dr. Johnson, Bob Evans,
Bishop Doane & Father O'Grady Roosevelt (T.)

Zsa Zsa Kennedy

Debbie & Billie Kennedy

President Theodore Roosevelt had critters big and small. Some of his family's favorites were five guinea pigs. The president named them after people he admired, including Admiral Dewey, Roosevelt's horse riding companion and the highest-ranked officer in the navy.

Admiral Dewey

Dr. Johnson

Bishop Doane

Fighting Bob Evans

Father O'Grady

The Roosevelts also had a couple of flying squirrels. Their names have been lost to history,

but they were known to hide in the Roosevelt children's pockets, waiting for lumps of sugar.

First Lady Louisa Adams, the
wife of John Quincy Adams, found
life difficult at the White House.

But she sought
comfort in some
tiny companions—
silkworms that she
kept on mulberry trees.
She harvested their silk and
spun it into fabric that she used
in her sewing projects.

Almost every president to call the White House home has found companionship
and comfort in a pet. Andrew Johnson was one of the few exceptions.

Even though Johnson didn't officially have a pet, one day some mice wandered into
his bedroom. The mice arrived while Johnson awaited charges of impeachment.

He fed them flour from his family's mill, addressing them as "little fellows." Watching their antics surely brought him peace and comfort during this uncertain time.

After all, even when you are leaving Washington, a friend is welcome.

A NOTE ABOUT TEXT AND ART

Whether or not Truman actually said "If you want a friend in Washington, get a dog" is anyone's guess. Maybe he did; maybe he didn't. But it is a great quote, isn't it? It should also be noted that some of the details surrounding the pets in this book (and the families they belonged to) have been lost to history. I have taken creative liberties throughout, but the stories are very much rooted in fact.

More about the presidents and their pets!

George Washington, 1789–1797
Dogs: Captain, Cloe, Drunkard, Forester, Lady, Mopsey, Rover, Taster, Tipler, Tipsy, Searcher, Sweet Lips, and Vulcan (all hounds).

Horses: Leonidas, Magnolia, Samson, Steady, Traveller, and other stallions, Blueskin and Nelson (Revolutionary War mounts), Rozinante, belonging to Eleanor "Nelly" Parke Custis Lewis, his step-granddaughter.

Bird: Polly, a parrot belonging to his wife, Martha.

Fun Fact: George Washington enjoyed hunting. He crossed French hound with black and tan hounds to create the American foxhound—the first official American dog breed!

John Adams, 1797–1801
Dogs: Juno and Satan (mixed breed), belonging to his wife, Abigail.

Horses: Caesar and Cleopatra (carriage horses).

Thomas Jefferson, 1801–1809
Bird: Dick (mockingbird).

Others: Two grizzly bear cubs, one sheep, and one ram.

Fun Fact: Jefferson was given two grizzly bears by general and explorer Captain Zebulon Pike. They traveled all the way from the West Coast on horseback.

James Madison, 1809–1817
Bird: Green parrot, belonging to his wife, Dolley.

James Monroe, 1817–1825
Dog: Spaniel, belonging to his wife, Maria.

John Quincy Adams, 1825–1829
Alligator: Allegedly. Records of the gator's whereabouts have been lost to history.

Silkworms: Belonging to his wife, Louisa.

Andrew Jackson, 1829–1837
Horses: Bolivia, Emily, Lady Nashville, Sam Patch, and Thruxton.

Bird: Poll (African grey parrot).

Fun Fact: Sam Patch (four-legged) was named after Sam Patch (two-legged), the first famous American daredevil, who in 1829 jumped from a raised platform into the Niagara River near the base of Niagara Falls.

Martin Van Buren, 1837–1841
A pair of tiger cubs.

William Henry Harrison, 1841
Cow: Sukey.

Billy goat.

John Tyler, 1841–1845
Dogs: A pair of wolfhounds and Le Beau (Italian greyhound).

Horse: The General.

Bird: Johnny Ty (canary).

James K. Polk, 1845–1849
No pets.

Zachary Taylor, 1849–1850
Horses: Apollo (a former circus performer) and Old Whitey (Mexican-American War mount).

Millard Fillmore, 1850–1853
Horses: Mason and Dixon.

Franklin Pierce, 1853–1857
Dogs: Seven small ones.
Two birds.

Fun Fact: Pierce received his seven small pups from U.S. Representative Commodore Matthew Perry after signing a treaty with Japan. We don't know for sure what breed the dogs were, but it is believed they were Japanese Chins, otherwise known as "sleeve" dogs because they fit comfortably in a kimono sleeve.

James Buchanan, 1857–1861
Dogs: Lara (Newfoundland) and Punch (toy terrier).
Birds: Two bald eagles.
Elephants.

Abraham Lincoln, 1861–1865
Dogs: Fido (who stayed in Springfield, Illinois) and Jip.
Horses: Belonging to his sons Tad and Willy.
Cats: Tabby and Dixie (and others, names unknown).
Bird: Jack (turkey).
Goats: Nanny and Nanko.
White rabbits.

Andrew Johnson, 1865–1869
No pets, but he did sometimes feed mice that wandered into his room.

Ulysses S. Grant, 1869–1877
Dogs: Rosie and Faithful (Newfoundlands), belonging to his son Jesse.
Horses: Butcher Boy; Cincinnati (saddle horse); Jeff Davis (wartime mount); Egypt and St. Louis (carriage horses); Julia (racing horse); Reb and Billy Button (Shetland ponies); and Jennie and Mary, belonging to his daughter, Nellie.
Birds: Parrot, and gamecocks, belonging to Jesse.

Rutherford B. Hayes, 1877–1881
Dogs: Dot (cocker spaniel), Duke (English mastiff), Grim (greyhound), Hector (Newfoundland), Jet (mixed breed), Juno and Shep (hunting dogs), and Otis (miniature schnauzer).
Cats: Siam and Miss Pussy (both Siamese) and Piccolomini.
Birds: Mockingbird and four canaries.
Others: Several carriage horses, cows, and a goat.

James Garfield, 1881
Dog: Veto (Newfoundland).
Horse: Kit, belonging to his daughter, Molly.

Chester A. Arthur, 1881–1885
Horses.

Grover Cleveland, 1885–1889; 1893–1897
Dogs: Collie, cocker spaniel, dachshunds, foxhounds, St. Bernard, and a poodle named Hector, belonging to his wife, Frances.
Birds: Canaries and mockingbirds, belonging to Frances, and gamecocks.
Ponies.
Imported fish.

Benjamin Harrison, 1889–1893
Dog: Dash (collie).
Billy goat: Old Whiskers, belonging to his grandchildren.
Opossums: Mr. Reciprocity and Mr. Protection.

Fun Fact: Old Whiskers pulled a cart carrying Harrison's grandchildren around the White House. One day the cart took off. People walking by the White House spotted the president running after the goat!

William McKinley, 1897–1901
Cats: Valeriano Weyler and Enrique DeLome (Angora).
Birds: Washington Post (double yellow-headed Amazon) and roosters.

Theodore Roosevelt, 1901–1909
Dogs: Pete (bull terrier); Rollo (St. Bernard); Sailor Boy (Chesapeake Bay retriever); Skip (mixed breed); Blackjack, aka Jack (Manchester terrier), belonging to his son Kermit; and Manchu (Pekingese), belonging to his daughter Alice.
Cats: Tom Quartz and Slippers.
Horses: Bleistein, Renown, Rusty, General and Judge, Jocko Root, Grey Dawn, Wyoming, Yagenka, and Algonquin (Shetland pony), belonging to his son Archie.
Birds: Eli Yale (hyacinth macaw), Loretta (parrot), barn owl, and Baron Spreckle (hen).
Snakes: Emily Spinach, belonging to Alice, and other snakes, belonging to his son Quentin.
Badger: Josiah.
Pig: Maude.
Others: Peter (rabbit); two kangaroo rats; flying squirrels; Admiral Dewey, Dr. Johnson, Bob Evans, Bishop Doane, and Father O'Grady (guinea pigs); plus a lion, a hyena, a wildcat, a coyote, five bears, a zebra, a one-legged rooster (plus other roosters), and a lizard named Bill.
Fun Facts: Tom Quartz was named after a character in a Mark Twain story, and Slippers was polydactyl (he had six toes on each foot). Roosevelt was said to have found the extra toes very amusing.

William Taft, 1909–1913
Dog: Caruso.
Cows: Mooly Wooly and Pauline Wayne.

Woodrow Wilson, 1913–1921
Dogs: Bruce (bull terrier) and Davie (Airedale terrier).
Cat: Puffins and Mittens.
Others: Songbirds, sheep, Old Ike (ram).

Warren Harding, 1921–1923
Dogs: Old Boy (English bulldog) and Laddie Boy (Airedale terrier).
Birds: Bob and Petey (canaries), belonging to his wife, Florence.
Squirrel: Pete.
Fun Fact: In honor of President Harding, newsboys across the country collected thousands of pennies to create a life-size sculpture of Laddie Boy. Harding was a former newsboy himself.

Calvin Coolidge, 1923–1929
Dogs: Bessie (collie), Boston Beans (bulldog), Calamity Jane (Shetland sheepdog), King Cole (Belgian shepherd), Palo Alto (bird dog), Paul Pry (Airedale terrier), Peter Pan (terrier), Prudence Prim and Rob Roy (white collies), Ruby Rouch (brown collie), and Tiny Tim and Blackberry (chows).
Cats: Tiger and Blacky.
Birds: Enoch (goose), Nip and Tuck (canaries), Old Bill (thrush), Snowflake (white canary) and a mockingbird, belonging to his wife, Grace.
Others: Billy (pygmy hippo), Ebenezer (donkey), Rebecca and Reuben (raccoons), Smoky (bobcat), Tax Reduction and Budget Bureau (lion cubs), a wallaby, and a black bear.

Herbert Hoover, 1929–1933
Dogs: Big Ben and Sonny (fox terriers), Eaglehurst Gillette (setter), Glen (Scottish collie), King Tut (Belgian shepherd), Pat (German shepherd), Patrick (wolfhound), Weejie (Norweigan elkhound), and Yukon (Siberian husky).
Alligators: Two, belonging to his son Allan.

Franklin Delano Roosevelt, 1933–1945
Dogs: Major (German shepherd); Meggie and Fala (Scottish terriers); President (Great Dane); Tiny (Old English sheepdog); Winks (Llwellyn setter); and Blaze (English bullmastiff), belonging to his son Elliott.

Harry S. Truman, 1945–1953
Dogs: Feller (cocker spaniel), and Mike (Irish setter), belonging to his daughter, Margaret.

Dwight D. Eisenhower, 1953–1961
Dog: Heidi (Weimaraner).
Bird: Gabby (parrot).

John F. Kennedy, 1961–1963
Dogs: Charlie (Welsh terrier); Clipper (German shepherd); Gaullie (poodle); Pushinka (mixed breed); Shannon (cocker spaniel); Wolf (Irish wolfhound); and Butterfly, White Tips, Blackie, and Streaker (puppies of Charlie and Pushinka).

Cat: Tom Kitten.

Birds: Bluebell and Marybelle (parakeets) and Robin (canary).

Hamsters: Debbie and Billie.

Horses: Rufus; Sardar, belonging to his wife, Jacqueline; Tex and Leprechaun (ponies), and Macaroni (pony), belonging to his daughter, Caroline.

Rabbit: Zsa Zsa.

Fun Fact: Zsa Zsa the rabbit was given to the Kennedy family by a magician—apparently she could no longer fit in the magician's hat! Her magic career came to an end, but it was rumored that she had another skill: she could play a toy trumpet.

Lyndon B. Johnson, 1963–1969

Dogs: Blanco (collie); Him, Her, Edgar, and Freckles (beagles); and Yuki (mixed breed).

Other: Hamsters and lovebirds.

Richard Nixon, 1969–1974

Dogs: King Timahoe (Irish setter), Pasha (terrier), and Vicky (poodle).

Fun Fact: Nixon had a very famous dog named Checkers while he was vice president—and Checkers might have saved Nixon's political career. In 1952, while campaigning alongside President Eisenhower as his running mate, Nixon was accused of taking illegal donations from supporters. He gave a speech defending himself and closed by saying that the only gift he had received was Checkers, and that the family was going to keep him. His approval rating soared.

Gerald Ford, 1974–1977

Dogs: Liberty (golden retriever), Misty (pup of Liberty), and Lucky (mixed breed).

Cat: Shan (Siamese).

Jimmy Carter, 1977–1981

Dogs: Grits (border collie) and Lewis Brown (Afghan hound).

Cat: Misty Malarky Ying Yang (Siamese).

Ronald Reagan, 1981–1989

Dogs: Fuzzy (Belgian sheepdog), Lucky (Bouvier des Flandres), Peggy (Irish setter), Rex (Cavalier King Charles spaniel), Taca (Siberian husky), and Victory (golden retriever).

Horses (at his ranch).

Fun Fact: Rex had the official job of turning on the power switch to light the national Christmas tree in 1985.

George H. W. Bush, 1989–1993

Dogs: Millie (English springer spaniel) and Ranger (one of Millie's pups).

Bill Clinton, 1993–2001

Dog: Buddy (Labrador retriever).

Cat: Socks.

George W. Bush, 2001–2009

Dogs: Barney (Scottish terrier), Miss Beazley (Scottish terrier), and Spot (pup of George H. W. Bush's dog Millie).

Cat: India, aka Willie

Cow (at his ranch).

Barack Obama, 2009–2017

Dogs: Bo and Sonny (Portuguese water dogs).

Donald Trump, 2017–

No pets.

Data courtesy of the Presidential Pet Museum.

Selected Sources

Calvin Coolidge Presidential Library and Museum

Presidential Pet Museum (presidentialpetmuseum.com)

Rowan, Roy, and Brooke Janis. *First Dogs: American Presidents and Their Best Friends.* Chapel Hill, NC: Algonquin Books of Chapel Hill, 2009.

Suckley, Margaret, and Alice Dalgliesh. *The True Story of Fala.* New York: Scribner & Sons, 1942.

Thomas Jefferson Encyclopedia (monticello.org/site/research-and-collections/tje)

Truman, Margaret. *White House Pets.* Philadelphia: David McKay Co., 1969.

Ulysses S. Grant's horse Cincinnati

Grace Coolidge & dog

Grace Coolidge & raccoon

Ulysses S. Grant's horse